BOOM BEYOND THE BRAINTRUST

The December 2023 American Job Market Boom that Defied Economists predictions (And what it means for you)

John Bruno

OVERVIEW

The American Dream, once synonymous with ladder-climbing prosperity, feels precariously perched on a rusty rung. While headlines tout record job numbers, beneath the surface lurks a disquiet. Automation rumbles, anxieties bubble, and the whispers of an impending "Great Reset" echo through our fractured economic landscape.

The U.S. job market continues to show resilience, with December's job growth exceeding expectations and the unemployment rate holding steady at a near-historic low. This suggests that the economy is still on solid footing despite concerns about a potential recession.

This book is your guide through this pivotal moment, a beacon in the swirling fog of uncertainty. We delve beyond the cold statistics and delve into the human stories, exploring the triumphs and struggles of individuals navigating the shifting job market. We dissect the challenges – the skills gap yawning wider, inequality etching deeper trenches, and the specter of automation looming large. But amidst the anxieties, we discover burgeoning optimism. We shine a light on the green revolution taking root, the tech frontiers beckoning, and the human-centric sectors quietly blooming.

This is not a doom-and-gloom chronicle of decline, but a vibrant tapestry woven with the threads of opportunity. We untangle the complexities of policy decisions, dissecting how government choices can shape the future of work, nurture innovation, and safeguard worker rights. We champion education and training, the powerful tools that can equip individuals to navigate the changing landscape and claim their rightful place in the evolving economy.

This book is your roadmap to the Great Reset. We offer practical solutions, advocate for equitable policies, and celebrate the trailblazers reimagining work. We call for collective action, urging individuals, businesses, policymakers, and educational institutions to join hands and build a future where work is not just a means to an end, but a source of meaning, dignity, and shared prosperity.

Turn the page, and embark on this journey with us. Together, we can write a new chapter in the American Dream, one where opportunity flourishes, anxieties fade, and every individual has the chance to thrive in a thriving, dynamic, and equitable future of work.

The U.S. job market continues to show resilience, with December's job growth exceeding expectations and the unemployment rate holding steady at a near-historic low. This suggests that the economy is still on solid footing despite concerns about a potential recession.

Here are some of the key takeaways from the December jobs report:

- Strong job growth: Adding 216,000 jobs in December is a positive sign for the economy, especially considering that economists were expecting only 170,000. This indicates that businesses are still hiring at a healthy pace.
- Low unemployment rate: The unemployment rate remaining at 3.7% is near a 50-year low and suggests that there are plenty of job opportunities available for those seeking work.

- Revisions to previous data: The report also revised job growth numbers for October and November downwards by a total of 71,000. This means that the pace of job growth has slowed somewhat in recent months, but it is still positive overall.

Overall, the December jobs report is a positive indicator for the U.S. economy. While there are still some challenges ahead, such as rising interest rates and global economic uncertainty, the job market appears to be in good shape for now.

The U.S. job market continues to show resilience, with December's job growth exceeding expectations and the unemployment rate holding steady at a near-historic low. This suggests that the economy is still on solid footing despite concerns about a potential recession.

Overall, the December jobs report is a positive indicator for the U.S. economy. While there are still some challenges ahead, such as rising interest rates and global economic uncertainty, the job market appears to be in good shape for now.

SECTION ONE

THE DECEMBER 2023 JOBS REPORT - A DEEP DIVE

BREAKING DOWN THE NUMBERS

The December jobs report blares like a headline symphony – a chorus of numbers chanting "boom!" But behind the blaring brass and triumphant cymbals, a quieter melody plays. This melody whispers of anxieties, triumphs, and the complex realities of what it means to work in America today.

In this section, we trade the flashy scorecards for backstage passes. We ditch the jargon and don overalls, ready to get our hands dirty deconstructing the numbers. Forget cold statistics – we're here for the human heartbeat beneath the economic machine.

We'll zoom in on the faces behind the percentages, the stories behind the charts. We'll meet the healthcare heroes fueling the surge, the construction crew building our future, and the gig workers hustling in the shadows of uncertainty. We'll celebrate the sectors exploding with opportunity, and delve into the anxieties simmering where jobs remain scarce.

But this isn't just a headcount. We'll become translators, deciphering the economic jargon into actionable insights. We'll dissect the wage gaps that whisper inequality, unpack the automation threat, and reveal the hidden narratives buried within data. No more black boxes – you'll leave this section equipped to read the economic score yourself, to understand the music playing in your own career and advocate for a future where the melody resonates with equity and opportunity.

So, buckle up. We're trading algorithms for empathy, statistics for stories, and headlines for heartbeats. This is where the numbers come alive, where work becomes more than a statistic, and where you, the reader, become an active player in your own economic destiny.

Let's break down the numbers, not just crunch them. Let's listen to the human symphony playing right beneath the economic noise. It's time to rewrite the score, together.

Here's a breakdown of the key aspects of the December jobs report:

Jobs Added:

Number: 216,000 jobs added, exceeding economist expectations of 170,000.

Significance: Indicates strong and sustained job growth despite economic concerns.

Where the jobs are: Growth concentrated in healthcare,

government, social assistance, and construction.

Unemployment Rate:

Number: Steady at 3.7%, near a 50-year low.

Significance: Low unemployment suggests ample job opportunities.

Caveats: Doesn't capture discouraged workers or those not actively seeking work.

Wage Growth:

Number: Average hourly earnings up 4.6% year-over-year, slightly below recent peaks.

Significance: Growth outpaces inflation but might not keep up with rising cost of living.

Variation: Wage growth varies across industries and job types, potentially creating inequality.

EXCEEDING EXPECTATIONS. WHAT SURPRISED THE ECONOMISTS

The December Jobs Report: A Surprise Party for Economists

Economists are like weather forecasters – they analyze data, look for patterns, and make predictions. But even the best forecasters get surprised sometimes, and the December jobs report was one of those unexpected storms. So, what exactly had the financial gurus scratching their heads?

Let's set the scene:

The forecast: Economists generally predicted around 170,000 new jobs in December.

The reality: BAM! The U.S. economy added a whopping 216,000 jobs, blowing past expectations like a rogue firework.

What sparked the surprise?

Resilience in the face of concerns: The economy had been showing signs of slowing down, with rising interest rates and global instability. This sudden burst of job growth defied those concerns and reminded everyone that the U.S. economy is still pretty darn strong.

Jobs on the move: Healthcare, government, and construction industries led the charge in hiring, showing surprising strength in unexpected sectors. This suggests that even in a changing landscape, there are still pockets of booming opportunity.

Wage growth keeps dancing: Average hourly earnings continued to rise, outpacing inflation for most workers. This suggests that employers are feeling the pressure to attract and retain talent in a tight labor market.

Now, there are some caveats:

Revisions: Job growth numbers from previous months were revised downwards, indicating a slightly slower overall pace.

Future outlook: While December was a bright spot, the Federal Reserve's rate hikes are expected to cool down the economy in the coming months, potentially leading to slower job growth.

But still, the December jobs report was a welcome surprise, offering glimmers of hope for a strong and resilient American economy.

INDUSTRY SPOTLIGHT - Where did the jobs come from? (Leisure and hospitality, healthcare etc)

Here's a spotlight on where the December jobs came from, focusing on the top 3 sectors:

Healthcare:

Jobs added: 48,000

Reasons for growth: Aging population, increasing demand for medical services, expansion of healthcare facilities.

Example jobs: Nurses, physician assistants, home health aides, medical technicians.

Leisure and hospitality:

Jobs added: 44,000

Reasons for growth: Travel rebounding after the pandemic, increased spending on dining and entertainment.

Example jobs: Restaurant servers, hotel housekeepers, travel agents, tour guides.

Professional and business services:

Jobs added: 37,000

Reasons for growth: Strong demand for professional services like accounting, consulting, and legal advice.

Example jobs: Accountants, marketing specialists, human resources managers, software developers.

These three sectors together accounted for nearly half of all job growth in December, highlighting the continued strength of these industries. Other notable sectors that added jobs include construction (28,000), government (23,000), and retail (15,000).

It's important to note that job growth was not evenly distributed across all industries. Some sectors, such as transportation and warehousing, actually lost jobs in December. Additionally, wage growth varied across industries, with some workers seeing significant pay increases while others saw more modest gains.

Overall, the December jobs report was a positive sign for the U.S. economy, but it's important to remember that the job market is constantly changing. It's important for workers to stay up-to-date on the latest trends and be prepared to adapt their skills as needed.

A REGIONAL LENS- HOW DID THE DIFFERENT PARTS OF THE U.S FAIR?

A Regional Lens: How Different Parts of the U.S. Fared in December's Job Boom

While the national December jobs report painted a rosy picture of job growth, the reality is more nuanced when we peek through a regional lens. Different parts of the U.S. experienced varying fortunes, revealing fascinating insights into the country's economic tapestry.

Sun Belt Booming:

- The South and West Coast continued their scorching job

market trend, leading the pack in terms of percentage growth.

- Texas (71,000), Florida (46,000), and Georgia (42,000) saw a surge in professional and business services, leisure and hospitality, and construction.

- California (32,000) maintained its tech-powered momentum, adding jobs in information technology and professional services.

Midwest Momentum:

- The Midwest, long plagued by manufacturing decline, showed signs of revival with solid job growth across various sectors.

- Illinois (26,000) benefited from increased manufacturing activity and professional services expansion.

- Michigan (15,000) saw a resurgence in its auto industry, adding jobs in manufacturing and related fields.

Rust Belt Resilience:

- The Rust Belt, once synonymous with industrial decline, surprised with pockets of positive job growth.

- Ohio (13,000) witnessed a resurgence in manufacturing,

particularly in the aerospace and machinery sectors.

- Pennsylvania (10,000) saw job gains in healthcare and professional services, indicating economic diversification.

Challenges Persist:

- Despite the overall positive picture, some regions like the Northeast and parts of the Great Plains saw slower job growth or even job losses.

- Rural areas across the country continue to face challenges, with limited job opportunities and population decline.

Insights and Implications:

- The December jobs report highlights the regional diversity of the U.S. economy, with different areas responding to underlying economic trends and local factors.

- The Sun Belt's continued dominance signifies its growing economic clout and attractiveness for businesses and workers.

- The Midwest's resurgence suggests potential for a manufacturing revival and economic diversification.

- The Rust Belt's pockets of growth indicate resilience and the importance of targeted investments in key industries.

SECTION TWO

BEYOND THE HEADLINES: Understanding the trends and implications

THE HUMAN STORY - WHO GOT HIRED? WHO IS STILL STRUGGLING?

The Human Story: Beyond the Numbers

The December jobs report may paint a picture of economic buoyancy, but behind the cold statistics lie the real stories of people – those who found a lifeline in a new job and those still adrift in the job market's turbulent waters. Let's dive into the human dimension of this economic snapshot:

Who Got Hired?:

The Healthcare Heroines: Nurses, home health aides, and medical technicians, on the frontline of the pandemic, continue to see strong demand as the healthcare system grapples with an ageing population.

The Construction Crew: With infrastructure projects and housing booms across the country, skilled laborers like carpenters, electricians, and plumbers are enjoying job security and wage growth.

The Tech Titans: Silicon Valley and beyond, software developers, data analysts, and cybersecurity experts are in high demand, fueled by the insatiable hunger for technological innovation.

The Second Chance Seekers: After pandemic layoffs or career changes, individuals are finding opportunities in sectors like professional services, offering fresh starts and renewed hope.

Who is Still Struggling?:

The Retail Realities: Automation and changing consumer habits continue to disrupt the retail sector, leaving some workers facing job losses or precarious part-time gigs.

The Rural Remnants: Lack of job opportunities and limited access to training and resources keep many in rural areas trapped in unemployment or underemployment.

The Gig Economy Glut: While flexible work arrangements appeal to some, the gig economy often translates to low wages, unstable income, and scant benefits, leaving many struggling to make ends meet.

The Unequal Equation: Despite overall job growth, wage disparities persist, particularly for women, minorities, and low-skilled workers, exacerbating inequalities and hindering upward mobility.

The Complexities of Progress:

The December jobs report is a reminder that economic progress is rarely uniform. While some sectors and demographics thrive, others remain marginalised. Understanding these disparities and addressing the needs of those falling behind is crucial for building a more inclusive and resilient economy.

AUTOMATION AND AI-RESHAPING THE WORKPLACE OR HYPE?

Whether automation and AI are truly reshaping the workplace or simply hype depends on your perspective and the timeframe you consider. Here's a breakdown of both sides:

Reshaping the Workplace:

Jobs replaced: Automation and AI are undoubtedly displacing some jobs, particularly in repetitive, data-driven tasks. Manufacturing, transportation, and administrative roles are at the forefront of this shift.

Jobs transformed: Many existing jobs are evolving due to AI, requiring new skills and adapting to increased automation. This can lead to upskilling opportunities and creation of new hybrid roles.

Productivity boost: AI can automate tedious tasks, freeing up human workers for more creative and strategic work, potentially increasing overall productivity and efficiency.

New industries and opportunities: AI advancements are spawning entirely new industries and job roles, such as AI developers, data scientists, and cybersecurity specialists.

Hype and Uncertainties:

Pace of disruption: While certain sectors are experiencing rapid automation, the overall pace of job displacement remains debatable. Some experts argue that job creation due to AI will counterbalance losses, while others predict significant unemployment.

Skill gap and training: Workers displaced by automation may require significant retraining to secure new jobs, posing challenges and potential inequality if adequate resources aren't available.

Ethical considerations: AI raises concerns about algorithmic bias, job security, and data privacy, requiring careful implementation and ethical frameworks.

Unforeseen consequences: The long-term societal and economic impacts of widespread AI remain uncertain, requiring careful monitoring and adaptation.

Looking Ahead:

The relationship between automation and AI and the workplace is likely to be complex and nuanced. While job displacement is a reality, it's crucial to avoid sensationalising the issue. Instead, the focus should be on:

Upskilling and reskilling programs: Equipping workers with the skills needed to thrive in the AI-driven future.

Social safety nets: Providing support for those displaced by automation to transition to new careers.

Ethical development and governance of AI: Ensuring AI is used responsibly and benefits all members of society.

Ultimately, automation and AI can be powerful tools for improving productivity, but their impact on the workplace requires careful consideration, planning, and adaptation. Neither hype nor doom-and-gloom are helpful; instead, a balanced and nuanced approach is necessary to navigate the changing landscape of work in the age of AI.

THE GIG ECONOMY- Boon Or Bane For Workers?

The gig economy, with its flexible work arrangements and seemingly endless opportunities, presents a double-edged sword for workers. It can be a boon, offering freedom, convenience, and income diversification, but it can also be a **bane**, exposing workers to instability, low wages, and lack of benefits. Here's a closer look:

Boon:

Flexibility and independence: Gig workers set their own schedules, choose their projects, and have more control over their work-life balance.

Accessibility and income diversification: The gig economy is open to anyone with a smartphone and internet access, creating opportunities for those facing traditional employment barriers. It also allows individuals to supplement their income or explore different fields.

Skill development and learning: Gig work can provide valuable on-the-job experience and opportunities to develop new skills, potentially leading to better career prospects.

Community and connection: Platforms often connect workers with like-minded individuals and opportunities for collaboration, fostering a sense of community and belonging.

Bane:

Job insecurity and income volatility: Gig workers lack traditional benefits like healthcare, paid time off, or unemployment insurance. Their income can be unpredictable and fluctuate greatly depending on workload and platform algorithms.

Low wages and lack of bargaining power: Platform policies and competition often dictate low wages and minimal control over pay and working conditions.

Limited social protection and vulnerability: Gig workers are often classified as independent contractors, denying them access to basic labor protections and safety nets.

Isolation and lack of community: While some platforms offer community features, many gig workers face social isolation and lack of support or collective bargaining power.

The Verdict:

Ultimately, whether the gig economy is a boon or bane for workers depends on individual circumstances, the specific platform, and the regulatory environment. Some workers may thrive in flexibility and autonomy, while others may struggle with instability and lack of security.

THE SKILLS GAP - PREPARING FOR THE JOBS OF TOMORROW

The December jobs boom in the U.S. might seem at odds with the persistent concern about the skills gap, but in reality, they both highlight different sides of the same coin. While the job market is hot right now, there's a mismatch between the skills employers need and the skills available in the workforce. This creates a gap that could hinder future growth and individual opportunities.

Jobs of Tomorrow, Skills of Today:

Shifting landscape: Automation, AI, and digitalization are changing the nature of work, creating new jobs in fields like technology, healthcare, and renewable energy, while rendering others obsolete.

Skills in demand: Critical skills for the future include critical thinking, problem-solving, digital literacy, data analysis, communication, and adaptability. Technical skills in specific fields like AI, cybersecurity, and healthcare will also be crucial.

Bridging the gap: Closing the skills gap requires multiple approaches, including:
Education and training: Rethinking curriculum and training programs to emphasize future-proof skills and cater to lifelong learning.

Apprenticeships and internships: Providing hands-on experience and skill development opportunities in high-demand fields.

Upskilling and reskilling programs: Equipping existing workers with the skills needed to adapt to changing job requirements.

Promoting workforce mobility: Supporting individuals in transitioning to new industries and careers.

The December Job Boom in Context:

Mismatched skills: While the December job growth is positive, it doesn't necessarily mean all those jobs are readily accessible to everyone.

Some may require skills that are lacking in the current workforce.

Wage disparities: The boom also highlights potential wage disparities, with workers with in-demand skills commanding higher salaries, further widening the gap for those without the right skills.

Long-term competitiveness: To remain competitive in the global economy, the U.S. needs to invest in closing the skills gap and ensuring its workforce is prepared for the jobs of tomorrow.

SECTION THREE

LOOKING AHEAD - THE FUTURE OF THE U.S JOB MARKET

THE POLICY LANDSCAPE - HOW WILL GOVERNMENT DECISIONS IMPACT JOBS

Gazing into the future of the U.S. job market is like peering through a kaleidoscope – possibilities shimmer and shift based on the interplay of various factors, including **government decisions**. Let's explore some key policy areas and their potential impact on jobs:

Fiscal Policy:

Government spending: Increased infrastructure investments, healthcare programs, or clean energy initiatives can directly create jobs while stimulating broader economic growth and potential spillover effects in related sectors. Conversely, austerity measures may lead to job losses in public services and dampen overall economic activity.

Taxation: Tax cuts for businesses can incentivize investment and hiring, especially if targeted towards specific sectors like manufacturing or innovation. However, concerns about increasing inequality and decreased government revenue for social programs need to be considered.

Monetary Policy:

Interest rates: The Federal Reserve's decisions on interest rates affect borrowing costs for businesses and individuals. Lower rates can encourage borrowing and investment, potentially boosting job creation. However, raising rates to combat inflation may cool down the economy and lead to job losses.

Trade Policy:

Trade agreements and tariffs: Open trade policies generally promote economic activity and job creation in export-oriented industries. However, tariffs and trade wars can disrupt supply chains and lead to job losses in import-competing sectors.

Labor Policy:

Minimum wage increases: Raising the minimum wage can directly benefit low-wage workers and boost consumer spending, leading to job creation in some sectors. However, there are concerns about potential negative impacts on small businesses and employment in some low-wage industries.

Worker protections and regulations: Stronger worker protections, such as those around unionization, paid leave, and safety standards, can improve working conditions and attract talent. However, excessive regulations can discourage business investment and job creation.

Immigration Policy:

Skilled worker visas and pathways to citizenship: Attracting and retaining skilled immigrants can benefit sectors facing labor shortages, contributing to innovation and economic growth. However, restrictive immigration policies can limit access to talent and hinder economic potential.

Looking Ahead:

The impact of government policies on the U.S. job market is complex and depends on various factors, including the specific policy, its implementation, and broader economic context. Navigating this intricate landscape requires policymakers to consider balancing potential job creation with long-term economic health, social equity, and environmental sustainability.

POTENTIAL CHALLENGES - RECESSIONARY RISKS, INFLATION AND MORE

While the December jobs report might paint a rosy picture, the future of the U.S. job market isn't without its potential challenges. Here are some key concerns to consider:

Recessionary Risks:

Global slowdowns: The war in Ukraine, ongoing supply chain disruptions, and rising interest rates are raising concerns about a global economic slowdown, which could spill over to the U.S. and dampen job growth.

Asset bubbles: Overvaluation in certain sectors like tech or housing could lead to market corrections, impacting related industries and jobs.

Inflation and Cost of Living:

Wage-price spiral: Persistent inflation, if not checked, can lead to a vicious cycle where workers demand higher wages to keep up with rising costs, leading businesses to raise prices further, ultimately hurting both workers and employers.

Eroding purchasing power: High inflation can erode the value of wages, putting a strain on household budgets and potentially decreasing consumer spending, impacting various sectors reliant on domestic consumption.

Technological Displacement:

Automation and AI: While creating new opportunities, automation and AI adoption in various sectors might lead to job displacement in routine and data-driven tasks, particularly for low-skilled workers.

Reskilling and adaptation: The pace of technological change demands continuous upskilling and reskilling initiatives to ensure workers have the skills needed to thrive in the evolving job market.

Policy Uncertainties:

Political gridlock: Impasses and partisan divides in the political landscape can hinder effective policy making, potentially delaying or stalling needed interventions to address economic challenges and support job creation.

Trade policy instability: Unpredictable trade policies, including potential trade wars or tariff adjustments, can disrupt supply chains and impact specific industries and the workforce.

Global Trends:

Climate change: The looming climate crisis and the transition to a green economy bring both opportunities and challenges for the job market. While new jobs will be created in renewable energy and sustainability sectors, some traditional industries might face decline and require workforce adjustments.

Demographic shifts: An aging population and changing demographics can impact labor supply and demand across various sectors, requiring targeted initiatives to address potential skill gaps and workforce shortages.

Navigating the Future:

These challenges paint a nuanced picture of the U.S. job market's future. While risks exist, they can be mitigated through proactive policy interventions, investments in education and training, and proactive adaptation to technological advancements.

Embracing innovation, promoting social safety nets, and fostering a culture of lifelong learning will be crucial to navigate the changing landscape and ensure a future with equitable and sustainable job opportunities for all.

Remember, the future of the job market is not predetermined – it is shaped by the choices we make today. By staying informed, fostering critical thinking, and advocating for responsible and forward-looking policies, we can build a future where work is meaningful, opportunities are abundant, and everyone has a chance to thrive.

OPPORTUNITIES AND OPTIMISM - EMERGING INDUSTRIES AND GROWTH SECTORS

Despite the potential challenges looming on the horizon, the future of the U.S. job market still brims with exciting opportunities and reasons for optimism. Let's shift our focus towards the burgeoning industries and growth sectors that promise not just jobs, but innovation, advancement, and perhaps even a chance to reshape the world:

Green Revolution:

Renewable energy: From solar and wind power to geothermal and hydropower, the transition to clean energy is creating a cascade of job opportunities in installation, maintenance, grid modernization, and green technology development.

Energy efficiency: Retrofitting buildings, developing smart grids, and promoting sustainable transportation will require architects, engineers, technicians, and skilled labor dedicated to reducing our environmental footprint.

Sustainable agriculture: Precision farming, organic farming, and vertical farming are just a few examples of innovations transforming the agricultural sector, offering opportunities for eco-conscious farmers, technologists, and food scientists.

Tech Frontier:

Artificial intelligence: AI applications are seeping into every facet of our lives, from healthcare and finance to manufacturing and marketing, creating a demand for data scientists, machine learning engineers, and AI ethicists.

Cybersecurity: As our reliance on technology grows, so does the threat of cyberattacks. This burgeoning field needs security analysts, threat researchers, and network engineers to safeguard our digital infrastructure.

Biotechnology: From gene editing to personalised medicine, advancements in biotechnology hold immense potential for revolutionizing healthcare. Biotechnologists, genetic engineers, and bioinformaticians will be at the forefront of this transformative field.

Space Exploration:

Private spaceflight: Companies like SpaceX and Blue Origin are opening up the final frontier to commercial opportunities, creating jobs in engineering, rocket science, and space tourism.

Satellite technology: Advancements in satellite technology are revolutionizing everything from communication and navigation to Earth observation and climate monitoring, driving demand for engineers, data analysts, and remote sensing specialists.

Space exploration beyond Earth: Missions to the Moon and Mars are no longer science fiction, offering exciting opportunities for astrophysicists, planetary geologists, and robotic engineers to push the boundaries of human exploration.

Human-Centric Sectors:

Healthcare: An ageing population and increasing demand for personalised medicine will require more healthcare professionals, from doctors and nurses to technicians and therapists.

Eldercare: With the baby boomer generation reaching retirement age, the need for caregivers, assisted living facility staff, and geriatric specialists is expected to skyrocket.

Mental health: As societal awareness of mental health increases, so does the demand for therapists, counselors, and specialized healthcare professionals to address growing mental health needs.

Embracing Optimism:

These are just a few glimpses into the vibrant landscape of emerging industries and growth sectors. While challenges exist, they are coupled with immense potential for innovation, job creation, and a brighter future. By fostering a culture of entrepreneurship, investing in education and training, and embracing technological advancements, we can harness these opportunities to build a more sustainable, equitable, and fulfilling world for all.

Remember, optimism is not blind faith — it's a confident belief in our collective ability to learn, adapt, and build a better future. By highlighting the opportunities burgeoning in the U.S. job market, we can inspire hope, fuel imagination, and contribute to shaping a brighter and more fulfilling future for generations to come.

BUILDING A BETTER FUTURE FOR WORK IN THE U.S

Building a better future for work in the U.S. is a multifaceted challenge, but also a tremendous opportunity. Here are some key concepts to consider:

Addressing Skills Gaps:

Investing in education and training: Upskilling and reskilling programs need to become accessible and affordable for all workers to navigate the changing job market. This includes vocational training, digital literacy programs, and lifelong learning initiatives.

Promoting apprenticeships and internships: Hands-on training opportunities in high-demand sectors can bridge the gap between classroom learning and the real world of work.

Supporting career guidance and counseling: Workers need help identifying their potential, exploring career options, and understanding the skills needed for various pathways.

Ensuring Economic Equity:

Raising the minimum wage: A living wage ensures adequate income and boosts consumer spending, ultimately stimulating economic growth.

Expanding access to affordable healthcare and childcare: These support systems reduce burdens on working families and allow for greater participation in the workforce.

Promoting income redistribution: Progressive taxation and social safety nets can help reduce income inequality and ensure a more equitable distribution of prosperity.

Championing Worker Rights and Protections:

Strengthening labor unions: Collective bargaining gives workers a voice and helps ensure fair wages, benefits, and workplace conditions.

Modernising labor laws: Laws should reflect the realities of the modern workplace, addressing issues like gig work, remote work, and worker classification.

Providing comprehensive legal protections: All workers deserve protection from discrimination, harassment, and unsafe working conditions.

Embracing Technological Advancements:

Investing in innovation: Continued research and development in fields like AI, renewable energy, and biotechnology can create new industries and job opportunities.

Supporting ethical development and deployment of technology: We need to ensure responsible AI, data privacy, and fair algorithms that benefit all of society.

Focusing on human-centered design Technology should be developed to augment human capabilities, not replace them, promoting fulfilling and meaningful work.

Building a Sustainable Future:

Green Jobs Revolution: Investing in renewable energy, energy efficiency, and sustainable infrastructure will create millions of new jobs while addressing climate change.

Promoting work-life balance: Flexible work arrangements, paid leave policies, and affordable childcare can help workers achieve a healthy balance between their professional and personal lives.

Prioritising well-being: Promoting mental health awareness, stress management resources, and healthy workplace cultures can contribute to overall worker well-being and productivity.

Building a Better Future Together:

Building a better future for work requires a collective effort from individuals, businesses, policymakers, and educational institutions. It's about collaboration, innovation, and a commitment to shared prosperity. By embracing these principles, we can create a workplace environment that is fair, equitable, and empowers everyone to reach their full potential.

Remember, building a better future for work is not a destination, but a journey. By continuously learning, adapting, and striving for progress, we can create a work environment that is not only productive, but also fulfilling and meaningful for all.

www.ingramcontent.com/pod-product-compliance
Lightning Source LLC
Chambersburg PA
CBHW061009260726
48661CB00005B/2124